WHEN THE WHOOPER SWANS CAME

When
The Whooper Swans
Came

Poems

Jane Picton Smith

First published in 2023 by Red Squirrel Press
36 Elphinstone Crescent
Biggar
South Lanarkshire
ML12 6GU
www.redsquirrelpress.com
in partnership with St Mungo's Mirrorball

Thank you to the Scottish Poetry Library for support from the Poetry Pamphlet Fund towards this project.

Layout, design and typesetting by Gerry Cambridge
e: gerry.cambridge@btinternet.com

Cover image: Pannawish/Shutterstock.com

Copyright © Jane Picton Smith 2023

Jane Picton Smith has asserted her right to be identified as the author of this work in accordance with Section 77 of the Copyright, Designs and Patents Act 1988.
All rights reserved.

A CIP catalogue record for this book is available from the British Library.

ISBN: 978 1 913632 51 9

Red Squirrel Press is committed to a sustainable future. This pamphlet is printed in Scotland by Love & Humphries using Forest Stewardship Council certified paper.
www.loveandprint.co.uk

Contents

Introduction / 7

The Archivists / 9
House on the Hill / 10
Black Bag Blues / 11
King Canute / 12
Jean Brodie and the Scotrail
       Train Announcement / 13
Poppies / 14
Dwelling of the Lady Poet / 15
Loch Machar / 17
When the Whooper Swans Came / 19
Before the Tide Turns / 21
The Bellbird / 23

Acknowledgements / 24
A NOTE ON THE TYPES / 24

Introduction

William (Billy) Bonar was a gifted and well-loved poet. He was also the co-founder of St Mungo's Mirrorball—the Glasgow network of Poets. He published three titles: his second pamphlet and full collection were published by Red Squirrel Press. Billy was a true altruist, one who always found time to support and encourage other poets in their work. Billy's second pamphlet, *Offering*, was published by Red Squirrel Press after he had won the James Kirkup Memorial Prize and was shortlisted for the Callum Macdonald Memorial Award. His first full-length collection, *The Stuff of the Earth*, was published just a few months before his death on the 15th of September 2021.

To mark his life and passing we were keen to create a poetry prize in his memory—one that offered a free opportunity to up and coming poets to have a pamphlet published and we were also keen to provide some mentoring support as well. We recruited Gerry Cambridge, poet, editor and founder of *The Dark Horse*, essayist, typesetter and designer, to design the pamphlet and work with the winner. The judging panel was also finalised and consists of Sheila Wakefield, Elizabeth Rimmer (Red Squirrel Press poet who also edits some of the poetry publications), Lynnda Wardle, writer and Billy's partner, Eleanor Livingstone (Artistic Director 2005–2010, Festival Director 2010–2021, StAnza) and Peter Mackay/Pàdraig MacAoidh (Senior Lecturer in Literature, School of English, University of St Andrews) who is our Gaelic judge.

The 2022 competition was launched along with Morag Smith's inaugural winning pamphlet, at St Mungo's Mirrorball on 16 November 2021. Again, it attracted a large number of high-quality entries and the winner was announced at St Mungo's Mirroball on 2 February 2022. The judges were again unanimous in selecting Jane Picton Smith as a worthy winner.

Jim Carruth, Chair, St Mungo's Mirrorball
Sheila Wakefield, Founder/ Editor, Red Squirrel Press

The Archivists

When we leave, it will be like this:
we'll fill up the tank and drive all night
until the seam of light
in the West becomes morning.
If we're lucky, we'll make Mallaig
and the dorsal fin of Eigg
on a clear day across the Sound.

Then, check into a sea-front hotel
ablaze with petunias and
other comforting clichés.
For dinner: 'Catch of the Day',
or maybe chips on the beach.
We might bicker over this,
or nothing, or think back to that
archived September of Rannoch Station,
of deer on the moor, receding into rain;
us deciding not to climb Schiehallion
and the sugar-white ghost of a church,
Our Lady of the Braes.
Unravelling like a heather root,
a vanishing point,
a library of days.

House on the Hill

Look at you, across the river,
dun walls hunkered,
set against the weather
just below the gorse line.
Close up, mud-blattered
by a passing tractor;
daubed in husks from
last year's wheat
—tawny if I'm generous.

We might share a gauzy watergaw,
smudged on the lip
of an unnamed hill, geese:
a broken necklace in the clouds;
domestic rites of pegging out
a chorus line of dancing girls
jostling for position in the gale.

Our lights might wink out code:
The dinner's made
My kids won't sleep;
so-called anonymity
laid before a stranger's gaze.

All this until we're gone,
even so, our homes stare on:
douce across the river.

Black Bag Blues

The black bin bag
is a bulbous crow
caught in the claws
of a sycamore tree
at the back of my
red brick Chiswick flat
on the track of the
District Line.

Some days it inhales,
impaled on the
unlichened branch,
all manner of diesel
and toxic emission;
a sorry condition
resigned to its
unending fate,
non-perishing state.

The day it takes flight
over rooftops and pylons,
I'll pack up my life
for Vancouver Island
where driftwood lies
smooth as bone,
or the tones of a
bluesy saxophone
in a place where
the coast road
takes me home.

King Canute

We weren't like the other mums
and daughters who flung their *love yous*
casually, as schoolbags over shoulders.
Instead, your love meant handing down
your learning like an heirloom,
what you knew of clouds and stars imparted;
wildflowers known and named:
lady's bedstraw, shepherd's purse.

Now that you repeat yourself,
repeat yourself, forget, I'll be like King Canute:
post myself, flint-faced, defend this futile beach
against the tide's increase, barter with the waves
to bide their time and leave for us a portion
of shoreline, an islet, a rock,
where we can talk of sea pinks
and forget-me-nots.

Jean Brodie and the Scotrail Train Announcement

I hadn't thought of her in years,
scarely past the Spring Term of '96
where, featured in the syllabus of
Scottish Lit, she proved her notoriety.

The last we heard of her in Edinburgh's
Morningside, the Braid Hills Hotel,
terminally ill, still desperate to caress
the spines of textbooks, magenta like
the rhododendrons in the gardens of EH4.

The tannoy states: *the next stop is Dalmeny,*
in schoolroom Scots, which interrupts the dull
commuter stupor of the Aberdeen-bound train.
I hear her name her *crème de la crème*:

Eunice turned a cartwheel,
Rose renowned for sex,
tragic Mary martyred
in the Spanish Civil War.

This unexplained ventriloquy, a turn of
Scotrail trickery, as we pass over kelp-happed
rocks to the latticed bridge at Queensferry.

People say they've seen her cycling
through Crammond, neat as a dahlia,
looking for her lovers
and the schoolgirl who betrayed her
in her prime.

Poppies

Encased in every green fur caul
year upon year
by the south-facing wall.
First, a glimpse of lips,
then we wake to a scarlet
explosion of paper blooms
so gorgeously un-ironed.
In the half-light, or the corner
of my eye, they're a company
of roosting macaws, flamboyant
as Frida Kahlo, kohl-eyed,
crimson and magnificent—
each seed-head like a well-baked pie.

Though my son cannot resist
the annual petal massacre, iconic
as the cover of a *National Geographic*,
in time they'll be spared
this beautiful carnage:
re-return, born again, allowed to fade;
each flower weighed
by the rain of future Junes,
until their season's end.

Dwelling of the Lady Poet

Frog Hoop Cottage, suggesting
culverts and disused wells
or the exodus of frogs
to a neighbour's pond
—perhaps a naiad's trick:
diverting water.

A knitted rainbow on the lintel
reminds us to be hopeful
and wards off plague.
LOVE in white letters framed
in the window.

No wonder you're inspired
with a garden full of sunflowers
—sanguine heliographers.
Their dinner-plate faces
trace the sun's course 'til dusk,
while each one vies for 'Best in Show'.

From your upstairs writing room,
Tibetan prayer flags festoon
like bunting on gala day.
Threads loosed by wind and August rain
unravel, fray and tangle
in the high branch of the birch.

Come spring, a wren may glean them
for her nest, a cobweb croched
in the wall, becoming green, red,

yellow, blue and white
by the pot-bellied chiminea
to sit oot on a starry night.

When the words don't come,
there are seed trays and potting on,
so much to do,
so much still left undone.

Loch Machar

In memory of Alexander Machar, a former Curator of Grounds and Gardens at Queen's College and then Dundee University from 1928–1968. He was the first to realise the potential of the Botanic Gardens site and his donated funds allowed the loch to be created in 1980.

More tottie than muckle,
your moniker suggests
a glacial remnant,
the rain-pail of some
less-kent glen.

Instead, you take your place
among the grand sequoias,
but while the public marvel
at the contents of a glasshouse,
you seem content with your lot,
your humble plot
of iris and aquatic ferns,
while cobwebs play cat's cradle
at your rim.

Like him,
your namesake, Sandy Machar,
a noted presence in these gardens;
Curator, planter, recounter
of learned Latin
for catalogues kept,
most happy handling earth
with sun-ripe hands.
In his time, a weather-teller;

you: a canny soothsayer,
dreich before a storm-pent sky,
while on a cloudless day,
you hold infinity.

When the Whooper Swans Came

They wintered here
the year before we came,
half-filled the field
so it resembled a partial thaw.
An incarnation of trumpet calls
and sudden flight:
sawing the air with oiled quills.

While sunlight stretched
in wingspans through our
empty, swept-out home,
we unpacked boxes,
laid down our own domestic
palimpsest of coupling
and bringing up of young.
In exchanges with neighbours,
we spoke of swans,
before our currency became
apples left beside the door
and bramble gin.

Though we keep a vigil,
they have not returned,
except a solitary pair,
a remnant,
an envoy from the North.
Perhaps they are no more than
a trick of the light,
twin ellipses of water
in the furrowed field.

Their flight path, a chosen diaspora,
over estuary and tundra,
leaves an imprint on
the territories of the mind.
Their departure:
a collective loss
that none can name.

Before the Tide Turns

If we were to beach our boat
on this crescent sandbank,
establish that the silt
would hold us,
then we might disembark
on this temporary islet
before the seals and waders
lay claim.

In the hull of our boat,
a football, for a game to last
however long the tide allows.
Daylight ebbs towards the Ochils
and the London train
becomes a glittering trinket
on the bridge,
throwing back vermillion suns
from every window.

It will soon be impossible
to tell outlying stars
from twinkling farms and steadings,
cooried in the hills:
Boötes the Herdsman
and the Plough.
We keep a keen eye
on the sandbank's shifting lines,
the diminishing pitch,
which will determine Full Time.

We don't keep score
adhere to any rules
except the chance to
flout the laws of Nature
before the current's twitch
pulls us back
into neat, unremarkable lives.
With that, we stow our ball
and row to shore.

The Bellbird

In the pines and eucalyptus,
the peal of your cathedral
praise recalls the aviary of
that room,
tuned to our wedding hymns.
Though we do not see
your shy, lime plumage,
the shadow of your flight
creates a shutter-blink
of interrupted light,
glorious chiaroscuro.

Our thoughts are tended
shrines within the forest.
Your syrinx: no bigger
than a tear.

Acknowledgements

'Loch Machar' was first published in *Our Botanic Garden:
A Place to Bloom*
(Dundee University Press, 2020).

'House on the Hill', *Poetry Scotland*.

'When the Whooper Swans Came', *The Lass O'Gowrie*, 2019.

'Before the Tide Turns', *Nutmeg*.

'King Canute', *The Hippocrates Prize Anthology*, 2021.

A NOTE ON THE TYPES

This book is set in Clifford Pro,
a contemporary serif designed by Akira Kobayashi
and available in three weights and six fonts.
Clifford Pro performs excellently in digital environments
and is a sturdy, versatile and beautiful typeface
suited to a large variety of text work, including poetry.
It received a Certificate of Excellence in Type Design in 2000.

The poem titles are set in Matthew Carter's rugged, slightly
sculptural sans serif Carter Sans, which makes
a useful companion face for the calm robustness of the serif.